Schist
Karen Smith

smith|doorstop

Published 2019 by
Smith|Doorstop Books
The Poetry Business
Campo House
54 Campo Lane
Sheffield S1 2EG

Copyright © Karen Smith 2019
All Rights Reserved

ISBN 978-1-912196-22-7

Designed and Typeset by Utter
Printed by Biddles Books

Smith|Doorstop Books are a member of Inpress: www.inpressbooks.co.uk. Distributed by NBN International, Airport Business Centre, 10 Thornbury Road Plymouth PL6 7PP

The Poetry Business gratefully acknowledges the support of Arts Council England.

Contents

5	Schist
6	Orthorexic Creed
8	How to Survive Blackgang Chine
10	Mr. Grey
12	Miss Etheridge
13	L'oeuf
14	Her
16	Ghost Train
18	Sunday Lunch, and yet
19	In Search of the Pepperpot
20	Poseidon's Trident
22	The Contortionist
23	Schizophrenia Test (amended for poets)
24	Driving in Iceland
26	Having Tea with you in the Orrery Café
27	Drawing Lesson
28	Burning the Years
30	Calling Pluto
32	Acknowledgements

For Carol & John Smith (1944 & 1945-2009)

Schist

One in a million, you said,
that summer at Mullion.
But we never could agree.
As we bickered all afternoon
between beach and lagoon,
the tide began to carry
more than it gave,
redrew the lines of flint
along the splay-veined shore.
Already, a boat was listing,
letting the water in.

Late lunch. We gorged ourselves
till the rivulets sang of home,
water scoring the mottled stone,
bathed like lizards. Double-spaced.
In the light, a certain angle of extinction,
fulsome but unforgiving. You told me
all you knew about the rock of the cove,
taught me something of the geology
of the heart. How the past leaves a mark.
I was distracted. But still, I recall
that twist of minerals, caked and forged
under an ocean of heat and torsion.
Dark amphiboles lit with feldspar and quartz,
forms that, despite all of time's weight,
retained their foliate planes, so easily
split. *Hornblende schist*, you called it.
I called it *slate*.

Orthorexic Creed

> *We believe in one God, the Father, the Almighty,*
> *maker of heaven and earth, and of all that is, seen and unseen...*
> – The Catholic Nicene Creed

We believed in John,
our father, the unsightly,
spectre of Croham Hurst,
who always walked, lean and unseen.

We believed it was right, Christ,
the only kind of love,
eternally forgotten by the father,
no word or song, night after night,
tuned out from tuning in,
forgotten, not savoured,
of one being with the illness.
By him all food was weighed.

For us kids and for our staycation
he came down from Croydon:
by the power of the catamaran
we stayed in caravans on the Isle of Wight,
and were made scarce.

For whose sake did his heart waste under the Hitler of diets?
He suffered death and was cremated.
On the third day he fared the same
in accordance with the victuals;
he ascended into heaven
and is seated at the opposite end to our mother.

He will pad again down the stairs to make his muesli and his bread,
and his Motown music will have no end.

We believe in the human spirit, the word, the singer of life,
who feeds on the morsels and the crumbs,
with the morsels and the crumbs he is sweet-tongued and super-sized.
He has broken through the shirt-cuffs.
We believe in one wholly catholic and bucolic girth.
We acknowledge one rhythm for the forgiveness of thin.
We look for the resurrection of the fed,
and the life in the words unsung.

Amen.

How to Survive Blackgang Chine

As you skip between the smuggler's blue thighs,
don't look up – it will look like the sky is falling.

Pretend you're lost in the maze again, though
the dead ends are the same and you're tall enough now

to see over the hedge. Try not to imagine the gorge
opening its jaws to you, that the landslides

are caused by some awakening beast that went
unnoticed, underneath, all these years while

you played. That the Blue Slipper is punishing you
for something you didn't do, while the tide runs off

with half the evidence. The clues are in the disasters
of the past: the shipwrecks releasing more bodies

on the rocks, the Weather Wizard who failed
to predict the rains that came to wash away

the cliffs. And him. Carry on staggering
round the black planks of the Crooked House,

grateful that you don't live like this family
of mannequins, on the tip of a latent crest.

Or recognise yourself in the Hall of Mirrors
with stick-legs, barrel heads, dead bug eyes.

Be pleased that all that's left of Buffalo Creek
is the photo of Ma and Pa, their dry smiles

at the saloon bar. Then, like Beauty, dreaming
to the taller edge of sleep, wake to find the ropes

unloosed and streaming free.

Mr. Grey

Smack! Like Pavlov's dogs,
we knew this meant
the start of English Lit.,
and as soon as your papers
hit the desk, until the pips,
we were yours.

At first I was less than impressed
by your pipe-smoking dress sense,
but I came to respect
your antique-shop air,
and after you played
The Great Gatsby in a sunny room
I couldn't help but see you afresh;
you were the convent school's answer
to Robert Redford, and I was hot for you,
Sir.

Oh Mr. Grey! You taught us
the meaning of *Macbeth*;
a language we could sense
but not properly decode,
let our voices roam right up to the drapes
of the school hall on drama afternoons,
your bottle-green two-pocket cardigan
appearing to sit and feast
like Banquo's ghost.

And there was more than a little kink
in the way you knuckled the wiry curls
of your tall fiery hair, in the exquisite
sighing arabesques
of your swash-and-flourish script.

It's difficult to say at which point I understood
stationery cupboards could assume
a bedroom aspect,
vertical and forbidden.
What makes these Levi's adverts so effective?
you asked.

Now I know.
Now I know.

Miss Etheridge

You rolled out of a storybook, between *Mary Poppins*
and *The Witches*. Masses of dark curls, a dimpled grin

and pockets full of party tricks. I rose above
the suburban cul-de-sac, over the school veg patch,

and into the worlds you painted with your words.
When, one afternoon, my eye swelled like a balloon,

I was afraid of turning into Violet Beauregarde,
right in front of my classmates. But you gave my eye

a name; a *sty*, and I drifted off again, wondering how a pig
could have got in. Rosie and I were flowers, you said,

both jostling for the light you were giving off. Who
could learn the flags of the world first? I only learned

how quickly the wind can change. "Your standards
have dropped," you said, "You're not as good as Rosie."

And what was wrong with the height of my socks?
I waited, but you didn't explain. That year the patch

dried up, and the seeds refused to split. Miss Etheridge,
I still think of you and your flags. The pig that got in.

L'oeuf

It was
a difficult
birth, she'd been
distracted. Dreaming
of helter skelters, 99 ice creams
and the gentle terraces of yesterday.
But it was the squawks of the wild geese
and the approach of human feet that made
her fluff her lines this time, spoiled this feathered
Barbara Hepworth's latest masterpiece, that lapped
like tides around her chalazae, spun on the earth's wonky
axis, the pissed magnetic fields that got her and Mr. Whippy's
love child drunk on the first breaths it drew of the universe.
Twenty-two hours of pushing, squeezing, creaming a calcium
caul the colour of the skin on cold tea from the warmth of her
rump. And all she's got to show for it is this Dutch tear of an egg,
ripe for candling, possibly dud, sealed before it settled in its cot,
more ellipsis than ellipse, far from eternal, riddled with ridges
and edges that didn't figure in the blueprints. Best laid plans
and all that. Still, one end's larger than the other, that's
what matters. This check may yet become chick.
If only we could make without breaking.
It's a wonder there's any talk
of which came
first.

Her

You walk up the white corridor.
Smile at the nurse. Fix my hair.

I am trying not to look like you
and not take offence at what everyone says.

This is what it means to hear hell.
They put me in one room, you in the other.

This time we hear the same sounds,
though they make a different message.

The pills help you realise that
voices have no bodies. You're real, mum,

remember to rise, eat and breathe
and you will not always be buried.

❋

You will always be buried,
forget to rise, eat, breathe.

Voices have bodies. You're not real, mum.
The pills help me realise that,

though they make the same message,
this time we hear different sounds.

They put me in one room, you in the other.
This is what it means to taste earth

and not take offence when everyone says
I am beginning to look like you,

smile at the nurse. Fix my hair.
I walk down the white corridor.

Ghost Train

Even before we clattered
into the blackness, I was
already there. Eyes shut,
head buried in your hair.

Ruffling and screeching like hens,
our bellies cracked like eggs.
My insides strained to escape,
to get between us and *them*.

"You're missing it, look!",
you elbowed me, but I'd seen
too many monsters already,
and the bangs, the bangs hurt.

No way of getting to the end
any faster. We were just dolls,
and nobody thought to make
anything to comfort *them*.

Yes, the skeleton might be crap
and home-made and just bones,
his wife smiling and beautiful
when she wasn't becoming a hag.

I still wondered, though, how
you could laugh so convincingly.
But you were older and brassier,
and now there's light enough,

you were the one
Mum shut in the cupboard,
the one who'd made friends
with the dark.

Sunday Lunch, and yet

there's no whiff of roast flesh,
no puff of Yorkshires,
no Waltons-style dining table.
This is no magnolia-walled feasting,
no "How has your week been, darling?"
and "Elbows off the table, girls",
no startled aunts with their wigs
slightly askew, marinating in their
cat-lady juices while they mop up gravy
with doorstop slices of granary loaf.
Oh no. No oven smoking in the corner,
no bitch fireside, licking her pups.
Just Dad's liver in the fridge, pooling.

In Search of the Pepperpot

Dark fret floods Chale cliff,
ghosts cows, oratory and sea.
Wrecked souls, pray for me.

Note: 'The Pepperpot' is the locals' name for St. Catherine's Oratory, Isle of Wight, the only surviving medieval lighthouse in England. A priest would tend the light and say mass for souls lost at sea. It frequently becomes obscured in bad weather.

Poseidon's Trident

Tunnelling under the buckle
of the island's chalk-belt,
we reach Alum Bay.
Fat with shipwrecks, rock-falls,
radio and rocket tests
and a battery of guns that sunk
more cliffs than boats
into the bay's night water.

The chairlift scoops us up,
swerves the potbellied cliff
and its ribs of quarried sand,
as we watch Dad's head bobbing
on the steps, taking out
his bread and his book
by the water.

A shingle spur clings
to the Needles' feet, trying
to become its own island,
the lighthouse slowly subsiding.
Prospero, still circling, has fallen
silent and each landslide recalls
Black Knight's gamma thrust,
and I think of the fissure that's opened up
in the crust at Headon Warren,
where the bodies are buried,

I remember my grandmother's tale
of a family picnic at the edge
when the hooves appeared above her.

Note: The title is a translation of the winning entry to a Chinese public vote to rename the Needles lighthouse, conducted by Visit Britain in March 2015. The form approximates the three chalk stacks emanating from the sea between the headland and light, known as the Needles. Prospero is a British-made communications satellite launched in 1971, part of the covert rocket-testing programme at the New Battery.

The Contortionist

Some nights, even the photos
come out slant. I'm Pinocchio,
except it's my spine that grows
the longer I lie with my body.
I channel my inner anaconda,
dismiss my hips in search of
the most incalculable angles,
and I'm back in the alleyway
of my thighs, looking to score.
The closer my knees to my ears,
the bigger the rush. Here comes
the impossible twist, the gasp,
the applause. I play my ribs
like a concertina, launder skin
until it folds, meek as towels,
and the heart tucks into the gap
behind the clavicle. I'm going for
a reverse birth, a fallopian curl,
ending in a fleshy haberdashery,
a sewing-up of the body
into the coat-tails, until
the audience can barely see me
and I almost believe I am
gone. Give this cat a box
and I'll fill every last inch, devour
each meaty crumb of black,
pulling the flaps behind me
until I reach that last, unbridgeable
crack.

Schizophrenia Test (amended for poets)

                       need to know
1) I feel that others ~~control~~ what I think and feel.

2) I hear or see things that others do not hear or see.

3) I ~~feel that it~~ is very difficult for me to express myself in words that others can understand.

  hope
4) I ~~feel~~ I share absolutely nothing in common with others, including my friends and family.

5) I believe in more than one thing about reality and the world around me that nobody else* seems to believe in.
                                                   * or only another poet

6) Others don't believe me when I tell them the things I see or hear.

              writing
7) I ~~can't~~ trust what I'm ~~thinking~~ because I don't know if it's real or not.

8) I have magical powers that nobody ~~else has or~~ can explain.

      don't
9) Others ~~are plotting to~~ get me.

                            job
10) I find it difficult to get a ~~hold of my thoughts~~.

             unread
11) I am ~~treated unfairly~~ because others are jealous of my special abilities.

  hear
12) I ~~talk to~~ another person or other people inside my head that nobody else can hear.

Driving in Iceland

                                                                            It   was   like

                          As if a lamp
            had fallen on its side

     The time after exams
     when we lay in a field

moment in the lab
       when the ray was

               As if we'd married
                    on the moon
                      and the sun

    As if this was the morning
     God caught his reflection in
              all along he had been

                            but his real work was

being born.

    leaking light.

           looking up
        at the sky. That

        split
           by a prism.

      was the only
        witness.

      and realised
  colouring in

in the leaving

Having Tea with you in the Orrery Café

At first we thought we were at the centre ourselves,
and everything spun around us. A kind of dance

where we just gazed in the mirrors at the others.
Forgot, even, to order any tea. Alice's Wonderland

as wallpaper to bigger and more luminous bodies.
The tables as reflections of their gyrations. Then

there were the postcards out the back. You know
the kind. This is a seaside town. Old habits.

The stars winking, like the night I lay with you
on the dunes. The Red King's hand holding it all.

It's best if you lie back, you said, admiring your face
in Jupiter of the jovilabe. *Slip a quid into the God slot*

and you can be like He-man, Master of the Universe.
Click. Whirr. The moon's Benny Hill whirl.

Drawing Lesson
after John Ashbery

First, draw the sea as it is,
not as you wish it to be.

Images can't be forced like rhubarb.
You'll be needing some light.

Don't think it, feel it,
like a blind person reading braille.

Imagine you're a child
wearing your eyes for the first time.

Seeing waves after naming them
is like attempting to soap the ocean.

Accept you can never fit it all in;
that's just the nature of the wave.

Treat the sea with respect.
Not everyone can be saved.

Burning the Years

Eleven miles and four centuries away
you lean over your furnace,
temples lit with sweat
as you sink your crucible,
casting nails, bells, fire-backs
and cannon. I wonder
why your tongue is so loose
in a time of such divide,
why you confess to the rector,
refuse to pacify Bishop Bonner
in the coalhouse, where he tortures you
with the kind of iron finery
forged by your own hand.

When they came for you at church
you fled, your bare soles charred
on the cinder path, cooled
on the stone steps of the tower,
then stood on the lip of the cornice
and gave your body to the wind.

Oh coz,
when they turned your flesh
to ashes you were my age,
and I hope you were
already commended to our God,
knew your name would live on
in this place, where burning
is more remembering now,

though beliefs continue
to dry until they catch.
The obelisk on the hill
has the best view in town,
and the steps you climbed
have been restored now. Come,
walk with me in the dark hours,
tell me what we don't share,
what we do.

Note: This poem pays tribute to Protestant martyr & East Sussex ironmaster Richard Woodman, brother of my paternal ancestor, who was burned to death in Lewes on 22 June 1557 as part of the Marian persecutions. This was the largest number of people burnt in England at one time and was intended to serve as a warning to others

Calling Pluto

After dark I call you up,
just to hear the weather report,
that the nights are drawing in now,
and how much you paid
for your latest pair of trousers.
You'll tell me the one about
PLUTO, the giant pipeline rolling out
under the Channel on a steel drum,
how it kept the tanks fed
for our boys on the continent,
how the ice cream hut along the bay
was really a pump in disguise,
like those Ruperts that kept the Führer
guessing. And the Kamikaze who'd blaze
unswerving to the end, the enemy
you couldn't help but admire. And I'll
sing you American Pie again,
like that last night in the hospital,
however many times you try to die.

Acknowledgements

I'd like to thank ...

For their support: my partner Michael Lucas and sisters Maria & Helen. Also to Alice Hiller, Emily Cross, Sonia Hope, Philana Bridgeman, Chris McCabe, John Davies, Anita Franchi and fellow writers and colleagues at Covent Garden Poetry Stanza, Lewes Live Literature and The National Poetry Library.

For their teaching & guidance: Carol Ann Duffy, Michael Woods, Mimi Khalvati, John McCullough, Saradha Soobrayen, Gary Mepstead, and Peter and Ann Sansom.

Thanks also to the editors of *Magma*, *Envoi* and *Under the Radar*, along with the staff at Moniack Mhor.

'L'Oeuf' first appeared in *Magma 68*, 'Poseidon's Trident' in *Envoi 180* and 'Schist' in *Under the Radar 22*. 'Schist' was commended in the inaugural Sussex Poetry Competition.